VIRTVTIBVS
MAIORVM
VT. SIT. OMNIBVS. DOCVMENTO. P.P.D.

Andreas Schäfler & Gabriela Wachter

LISBON

The Sparkling Miracle on the Western Edge of Europe

LISBON

The Sparkling Miracle on the Western Edge of Europe

There are many sound reasons for calling the Portuguese capital cosmopolitan. But just how many other cities of this rank can also boast that they are a feast for the eyes?

Lisbon owes this favour just as much to its topographical position as to its impressive architectural character. Located on the seven hills before the estuary of the Tagus River (Rio Tejo), the city took on its unequalled form over the course of many centuries. Despite serious setbacks caused by devastating plague epidemics, numerous earthquakes and other destructive catastrophes, a cityscape has developed which is brimming with history and continually enriched by elements from each new period.

In the first hours of his stay many a visitor toys with the idea of settling down here, because this city is so unassumingly charming. But unfortunately, prominent areas of the city centre are presently being lavishly restored with much ado, in an attempt to dress up the diva. In the periphery, choice areas have already been transformed into large construction sites, since Lisbon, which was Cultural Capital of Europe in 1994, is preparing itself for the World's Fair EXPO in May 1998.

left page:
View of the Igreja and Miradouro da Graça

Praça da Figueira and Rossio

A little like the two chambers of a heart, Praça da Figueira and Rossio are the focus of all the pulsating activities of the inner city. On these directly neighbouring main squares on the northern end of the lower city, numerous tram and bus lines start and finish. The squares are filled with honking taxis, clattering mopeds and people. From the early hours until late in the day the city bustles with life. But in the midst of all this movement, there is always time for a short break, and where better than in one of the three most famous coffeehouses in Lisbon: the Pastelaria Suica, the Café Nicola or the Confeitaria Nacional. The equestrian monument of King João I on the Praça da Figueira, hidden under a big Christmas tree in the wintertime, is also a favourite meeting place, and not just for pigeons. The main entrance to the central Rossio underground station is adjacent.
You reach the impressive square of the same name either by taking a small arcade lined with old-established speciality shops, or by passing the much visited Igreja de São Domingos. The very imposing National Theatre, the porch of which these days provides shelter for the homeless, was built in a distinctively classical style in 1842. It stands on the site of the Palace of the Inquisition, which collapsed in the great earthquake. The sentences of this institution were often carried out publicly on the Rossio.
Officially the square is still named after King Dom Pedro IV, whose bronze statue towers above the square on a marble column that is more than 20 metres high.

left page and right:
Praça da Figueira with old-established speciality shops in Lisbon's city center

ESTAÇÃO

left page:
Neo-Manueline portal of
Rossio Station
below:
Rossio Fountain between the
National Theatre and the
Monument of Dom Pedro IV

First Impressions
Chiado

When EXPO finally opens it will have been ten years since the city appeared in the international headlines – but for very different reasons. On the 25th August 1988 a fire raged non-stop for 24 hours in Chiado, the old business quarter between the lower and upper city, threatening large areas of the old city and in the end destroying three complete city blocks and two dozen elegant buildings in all.

Reconstruction, which only began in 1991, still continues to this day. Numerous concessions, mostly due to complications of ownership, had to be made by Alvaro Siza Vieira, Portugal's most renowned architect. The originals included not only a faithful reconstruction of the façades, but also the creation of affordable housing, which would have brought with it a long overdue revitalisation of the quarter.

In the meantime it is nevertheless predictable that this "problem zone" will eventually become Lisbon's Fifth Avenue. The intersection of Rua do Carmo and Rua Garrett, a marriage of reason between the glorious splendour of the past and the bursting self-assurance of today's elite, will be packaged as a marriage of love. More directly, the project is subsidised to the hilt.

On the upper end of the construction site fence decorated with historical photos and facing the Largo do Chiado, a patron saint turned to stone watches over his old beat from an immovable base, and unless appearances deceive, more than a little amused. Antonio Ribeiro, a Franciscan monk in the sixteenth century, indulged more in acting and poetry than in church services and became known as "Chiado". A few short steps away Fernando Pessoa is posed, cast in precious metal. A bronze statue of the poet, unrecognised during his own lifetime, was installed in front of "A Brasileira", once one of his favourite cafés, on the occasion of his 100th birthday in 1988. It was later temporarily removed to permit construction work.

left page:
Elevador Santa Justa
below:
In "A Brasileira"

The next step on our tour through the inner city and its history is the Elevador Santa Justa, which in many ways fulfils all the expectations of a veritable tourist attraction. This iron construction dating back to 1901, is approximately 40 metres high and decorated with filigree. While often attributed to Alexandre Gustave Eiffel, it is actually the work of Raoul Mesnier de Ponsard, a Portuguese engineer, albeit of French descent. In the tower of the Carmo-Elevator, as the lift is also called, two sumptuous cabins for 25 people each defy the 32 metres between the lower city and the Largo do Carmo.
Let your gaze wander from the upper platform of this somewhat curious landmark and you will be richly rewarded. Lisbon's impressive panorama of hills rises above the shadows of the ravine-like streets. Directly under the viewing terrace the burnt-out quarter of Chiado seems to bare its hollow teeth, since although the façades remain, everything else is thoroughly gutted. The pedestrian bridge from the platform to the Largo do Carmo is now unfortunately sealed, and the bizarre skeleton of the Gothic Carmo Church is slowly being restored. Its construction was begun in 1385 after the victorious battle of Aljubarrota that secured Portugal's independence from Castile. Largely destroyed in the great earthquake of 1755, it was preserved as a memorial and today houses the Archaeological Museum of Lisbon in its inner courtyard and the rooms of the former Carmelite monastery.

Igreja do Carmo

O R G A

CASA DA

CAIXA
TOP

The Heart of the City

Baixa

November 1st, in the year 1775 marks one of the most important dates of the history of the city. The ground shook all over the world, but the epicentre was in the middle of Lisbon. At that time the city was considered the richest in Europe and had 270,000 inhabitants. Over 50,000 died in the earthquake itself or in the resulting fires and tidal waves from the Tagus. According to geophysical estimates this catastrophic earthquake must have reached a strength of 8.5 or 9 on the international Richter scale. Hundreds of historical buildings and architectural monuments collapsed. Of those that had only recently been constructed, only the aqueduct, which is still used for its original purpose, and the Palácio dos Necessidades, which has since become the seat of the Foreign Ministry, remained standing. With few exceptions however the city centre appeared totally destroyed; only the Alfama quarter on the eastern edge of the castle hill was spared.

Never before had a prosperous flourishing metropolis been struck by a natural catastrophe of such vast proportions, and even the horror over the destruction of Pompeii had not spread as quickly or as wide. All of Europe was in shock. As can be gauged from the reactions of the great thinkers of the time, the myth of the feasibility of everything

left page:
Rua Augusta and Rua da Prata
above:
A pavement mosaic in Rua Augusta
below:
The Earthquake of Lisbon, engraving by J.C. Krüger 1774.

suffered a serious setback. Goethe, young Kant, Rousseau and above all Voltaire concerned themselves, each in his own way, with the social and political effects of the catastrophe. Voltaire's version in "Candide" was especially decisive.

In the defiant hope that bad could be balanced with good, all available forces were put into action as quickly and resolutely as possible. José I entrusted his power-conscious prime minister, the Marques de Pombal, with the reconstruction. And in fact, within a very short time this rabble-rouser carried out the royal order to "bury the dead, care for the living and close the harbours". With foreign financial help and dictatorial methods, he achieved daring and drastically progressive results. Already in 1760 a completely new quarter, built to a grid plan, with five-story buildings over cellars, was ready for occupation. The spirit of enlightened absolutism had overcome an acute emergency and had created a forward-looking model. This plan of an ideal city, the first of the modern era to be comprehensively realised, would soon be revered world-wide.

When the Baixa calms down...

The lively Baixa area, extending from the main Rossio and Praça da Figueira squares as far as Praça do Comércio, has remained Lisbon's business quarter up to today. Its potentially hectic pace is guided along quaint paths by the severe structure of the quarter. All forms of traffic are literally imaginable here; day in and day out they are set in almost theatrical competition, with spirited contests between car and tram, against a backdrop of relaxed pedestrians strolling along the Rua Augusta, seeking bargains in the shops that are still partially grouped by guilds.

The façades and interior furnishings of many old shops have remained virtually unchanged since the eighteenth century and in some places the scene seems so timeless that you could expect any moment to meet up with the absent-minded arts correspondent from the novel "Pereira Declares", with which the Italian Lisbon-expert Antonio Tabucchi had so much success three years ago. Or the assistant book keeper Bernardo Soares in Fernando Pessoa's "Book of Disquietude". Or even the writer Pessoa himself, who might be heading for his favoured local café Martinho da Arcada. This is

Lipton
PEPSI

E CAFE
278
CASA CHINEZA
O MELHOR
BOLO - REI
AR CONDICIONADO
CASA CHINEZA

the only bar which has managed to hold out in the busy pedestrian zone under the high arches of the Praça do Comércio until today.

above:
Praça do Comércio with the Equestrian Monument of José I
below:
Panorama of churches above the square
right page:
In the half-shadows of the arcades

Vorstellung und Beschreibung des ganz erschröcklichen Erdbebens, wodurch die Königl. Portugiesische Residenz-Stadt Lissabon samt dem grösten Theil der Einwohnern zu grunde gegangen.

Description of the most horrible Earthquake, by which the Royal Portuguese Residence-City Lisbon along with a great Part of its Inhabitants were destroyed.

Lisbon, the Capital of the whole Kingdom, a City, which contained more than 30,000 Houses, the most magnificent Palaces, and indescribable Riches, and was famous in all of Europe for her Beauty and her all-encompassing Business, Lisbon is almost no more. Only her Sites testify of that Glory which they previously were, but now have ceased to be. For on the 1st of November of this 1755th year of Our Lord, on the Feast of All Saints, exactly at the Hour in which a great Part of the People was come together in the Churches, it pleased the highest Judge to strike not only the whole Kingdom of Portugal, but principally the Residence-City with such Wrath that this City, with all its Palaces, Public and Private Buildings, Convents, Monasteries, Cathedrals and Churches, was transformed in two or three Minutes into a Pile of Stones by a Very Severe Earthquake which came to pass at around ten o'clock in the Morning. Only the College of the Society of Jesus, the Benedictine Monastery and the Monastery of the P.P. Carmelites remained standing; the Church of the latter is so badly damaged that the Service can not be held therein; all the other Houses of God are devastated and ruined. Innumerable People, Part of whom were in the Churches and the other Part of whom had run into the Streets to save themselves, were buried alive under a Shower of Stones and collapsing Walls. Of the Holy Men and Women of the Convents or the Canonesses who were praising God in the Choir, two-thirds are dead, and of 200 P.P. Franciscans no more than 30 or 40 survived. In many Churches almost all of the People present were crushed to Death by the Vaults that had fallen on them. In the Middle of this unbelievable Disaster the Terror was increased by a very violent Fire that began almost at the same Time and that was even more dangerous because nobody thought or dared to defend themselves, but in Fear of Death each Person requested only Confession and Absolution. Indescribable Treasures, as well as almost all Household Goods, Supplies, Business-Goods, and all Archives and Documents were consumed by the Flames. The Papal Nuncio saved himself as if by Miracle; but the Spanish Ambassador was crushed and his Body has not yet been found. The Inquisition-Palace was also consumed. Count Ribera, betrothed with Donna de Lucos, had scarcely before received paternal Permission to return home to marry his Beloved; the Wedding took place on the Day of the Disaster. The Groom saved himself, his Father and his Bride on a Ship; but no sooner had he thanked God for his Fortune, the Sea-Fury threw this Ship far inland and sunk it into the Earth. Upon hearing that in this Moment so many of his Subjects had perished, the King desired to rush to Lisbon from his Palace of Pleasure in Belém, located about a Mile from there; but what could the royal Presence have done for the unfortunate City? A sad Circumstance for so gentle a Monarch! He was beseeched and implored not to put His so very dear Life in Danger, for the Comforting of His Subjects. With a great Sigh His Majesty was eventually persuaded to stay behind, and waited, plagued by the deepest Pains, for three Days in His Carriage. What a moving Sight for the King it would be, were He to come to Lisbon! Collapsed Walls; open Spaces where Stones are piled up; Abysses that here and there are still open; a Handful of Citizens without Shelter; royal Subjects who run up to the sovereign Lords with pitiful Wailing; Limbs of mutilated Corpses spat out again by the Earth; Bodies of Human-beings and Animals which were mashed under the Rubble, lumped together and stacked up; Infants who were crushed at their Mothers' Breasts; despairing Fathers, surrounded by dying Children, unable to find Aid. Even among those who had extracted their Life from the Rubble like a Treasure, most of them are totally impoverished because of collapsed Supply-houses and Warehouses. For Centuries one had not heard of a comparable Earthquake; but it is also going to take many, many Years of hard Effort and Work to restore Lisbon to its former Glory, if it is at all possible. The royal Generosity is now Portugal's only Refuge. From its Income it will be possible to somewhat repair the Damage, with a Total of about 18 Hundred Million per Year. In the meantime an incredible Number of Tents have been raised around this unfortunate City, under which the Big and the Little, the Spiritual and the Secular alike are endeavouring to survive in Safety. We end this Story with the following Thoughts:

Not Aeolus' Breath, but the Creator's Hand of Judgement,
Nor Vulcan, but God himself with Avenger-Flames, Storm over you together, o Lisbon!
And that which does not collapse and fall will be miserably burnt.
O Lord! before whose Nod even Rock and Mountains shake, before Whose Breath even Flood and Waves rise,
How terrible is your Court of Wrath!
It would only take a Quarter-hour of Weather, before the Earth is sunk! and where is then our Rescuer?
And you, o Man! Tremble not.
You Mockers be silent, forget your Scorn!
God vanquishes, and all of Europe shakes!
Proud Cities hesitate! and feel it in your Crown!
Who knows when his Wrath will bury you in Rubble and Horror?
Not only Lisbon harbours Sinners,
The Arm of the Highest One punishes them all, here later, there sooner.

Contemporary leaflet, Augsburg 1755, Georg Caspar Pfauntz

Enchanted Labyrinth of Narrow Streets

Alfama and the Castle

We now turn to the temptation which presented itself from the Elevador Santa Justa: the Alfama. Whether by foot or on tram line 28, which after crossing the Baixa in an easterly direction climbs the first hill with a running start, the route is always uphill. First we pass the massive medieval cathedral Sé Patriarcal, Lisbon's oldest church.
The origins of the Romanesque church go back to the twelfth century. After the defeat of the Moors by Portugal's first king, Afonso Henriques, a new church was erected on the site of the mosque. The Moors were driven out of the Alfama and settled in the area that is still known today as the Mouraria after these early inhabitants. New archaeological finds in the Sé Patriarcal go as far back as to the fourth century and prove that even the Moors built on foundations that were already standing.
A visit to the church is especially worthwhile because of the light-filled cloister, in the chapels of which unpretentious treasures are kept, such as a Romanesque wrought-iron gate and a fresco from Visigothic times. Close-by a picturesque group of cleaners goes about its work: a dozen women and men crouch over excavation fragments and scrub them patiently with toothbrushes until they shine.
Two bends further up the hill you reach the Miradouro Santa Luzia, one of Lisbon's most beautiful vantage points. No other place provides a more revealing vista of the village-like structure of the

previous double-page, left page and above:
Views from Miradouro Santa Luzia
left: Some details

Alfama's disorderly growth. Its name, like almost all words beginning with this syllable, is of Arabic origin and refers to the warm springs that once bubbled here.
After this bird's eye view, descending the stairs of the Rua Norberto Araujo into the maze of narrow streets and confronted with the dice-sized houses from close-up, the impression of the Alfama begins to dissolve into a thousand tiny mosaic stones. The magic of patios decorated with flowers, the confusing array of smells and sounds, and not least of all the almost complete absence of motor traffic contribute to a panorama of everyday life that sometimes hardly seems to belong to the present. Here and there this idyll gives way to bitter poverty and the marvellous colours become monotonous, but the enticing side of this labyrinth asserts itself and cancels out the rules of spatial and temporal orientation. But just when you begin to feel that you have possibly just lost your way, curiosity and the spirit of discovery come alive.
The sudden juxtaposition of poverty and splendour, of public and private is especially visible in the Alfama quarter. Even here there are magnificent villas, respectable administrative buildings and guarded army barracks, sometimes right next to an almost stormily frequented pastelaria, that in addition to coffee and pastries also offers a whole

Mosaic of views of Alfama

assortment of other everyday necessities. In the long Rua de São Pedro there is an open-air fish market every working day, and a few blocks further a public wash-house is frequented in the same manner. In one or the other restaurant fado music is heard at night, and every June 13th there is a big festival. It is dedicated to St. Anthony, who was born in the Alfama in 1195 and died 36 years later in the city of Padua in Italy. Anyone who on this occasion has tried to find himself a spot on the steps that are so welcoming during the day or on the cosy terraces knows how passionately St. Anthony has been reclaimed for Lisbon.

The Castelo de São Jorge towers one level above the Miradouro Santa Luzia – that is, three or four steep streets further up this hill. This fortified castle, a striking eye-catcher in the cityscape, has alluringly lovely grounds that offer a magnificent view of the jumble of houses, the harbour, the Tagus, the 25th of April Bridge and the riverbank on the opposite side. High above the hills the towers of Lisbon's main churches ring out to each other. In the east-west axis the snow-white dome of the

Distinctive façades in harmonious competition

right:
The Cathedral Sé Patriarcal
rises above the Casa dos Bicos

above:
Castelo de São Jorge
below:
View of the jumble of houses
from the castle

Basilica da Estrela dominates as a distant goal behind the jumble of skyscrapers in Amoreiras.
The extensive castle grounds are richly steeped in history. Lisbon's urban development began from this hill. In the eighth century North African conquerors built a magnificent palace that was later rebuilt in the Gothic style. The castle served as residence for numerous Portuguese kings, until it was decided at the beginning of the sixteenth century to take account of Lisbon's development into a metropolis of world trade by building a new royal palace close to the harbour on the Terreiro do Paco, the present Praça do Comércio. From then on the castelo was used as a barracks and a weapons arsenal, until it fell victim to the great earthquake in 1755. It was not until 1938, under the dictatorship of Salazar, that a rather free historical reconstruction of the castle wall and its fortification towers was begun.

The walls and ruins of the castle are a green oasis high above the city

Miradouro Nossa Senhora do Monte

The eye adjusts to surprising contrasts

A Look at Opposites
Graça

To the Northeast of the fortress, the things that flattered all the senses from the Alfama upwards as well as in the tiny Mouraria quarter begin to disappear slowly and reluctantly, changing into the rather sober normality of the periphery. We have reached the Graça quarter. To be sure, you can still enjoy a very beautiful view of the hill with the castle from the miradouro of the same name. But because of restoration work, the nearby Graça church with its heavily damaged Baroque façade cannot be visited at present. Also the monastery that belongs to it is unfortunately even more permanently sealed-off, since it has been used as military barracks for a long time.

Igreja and Miradouro da Graça

The tremendous building of the "Voz do Operario" in the street named after it is definitely worth a side-trip, and not just because of the architecture. In the former headquarters of Portugal's socialist workers' association, which had become more and more important after the general strike of 1871, the organ of the movement, the newspaper "Voice of the Worker" was produced. In addition it served as a social and cultural meeting place for all of the city's workers. Even today the classically trimmed art nouveau building still echoes with loud, high voices, at least during the day. Kindergartens and a cafeteria remain in use, but the "Voz do Operario" has fallen silent in its archive.

Workers' housing is still to be found in the nearby catchment area, for example to the north of the Largo da Graça. Preserved behind the façades of the main buildings, decorated with tiles and balconies, which were naturally reserved for the families of the factory owners, are several of these two- to three-story housing blocks from the turn of the century. Perfect examples are Vila Berta and Vila Rodrigues, both in the Rua do Sol a Graça, in which the individual apartments are joined to each other by complex veranda constructions around a spacious patio.

An absolute must, before we start downhill to the

View of the castle from the Miradouro da Graça

One of Lisbon's would-be symbols

east end of the old city once again, is a visit to the vantage point that brings us closest to the heavens over Lisbon. On the nearly precipitous summit of the Graça-hill and fully exposed to the elements is the Miradouro Nossa Senhora do Monte. From here you can see the parts of the city that face the river, all the way back to their frayed edges in the distance. And even the 2.3 kilometre long Tagus Suspension Bridge and the 100 metre high statue of Christ on the opposite bank of the river can enrich the scenario with emotion and splendour.
Not far removed is the first real slum, a settlement of crooked barracks on a downward sloping plot of formerly uncultivated land. The inhabitants fetch their water from the nearest hydrant. For more and more new Lisboans who do not find a place in the isolated tenement blocks of the lowest standard, there is no other choice than this improvised kind of survival. Besides campaigns to legalise the occupation of these camps, the Portuguese state has hardly anything to offer to this marginal group. Just a few steps from here, an unexpectedly showy, new pink building towers al-

most scornfully on the horizon. It is a post-modernist howler and provocative warning, one of the many would-be landmarks that have recently sprung up in the Lisbon area.
Our excursion ends with a walk through the fantastically positioned Rua Senhora da Gloria which leads into the grand market place between the church and abbey of São Vicente on the right and the Pantheon Santa Engrácia on the left side. This massive domed building is unique, if only because of its long construction time. After the foundation-stone was laid more than 300 years ago, it was not completed, believe it or not, until 1966 under the rule of Salazar, who immediately designated it as the worldly hall of fame for Portuguese citizens of outstanding merit. Indeed the severely symmetrical Renaissance ensemble of the neighbouring São Vicente church comes close to this. In the refectory of this former Augustinian Abbey the sarcophagi of almost all the members of the royal Bragança dynasty have been kept since the middle of the last century, watched over by an angel of stone.

Igreja-Panteão de Santa Engrácia

In the Mosteiro de São Vicente

Monumental Lisbon:
The 25th of April Bridge and
the Statue of Cristo Rei

A last look back into
the narrow streets of Graça
from the Largo Martim Moniz.

Circuit through the Western City

Bairro Alto, Rato, Estrela

From the Rossio we cross the Praça dos Restauradores and walk past the venerable Avenida-Palace-Hotel and the Rossio-Station, both of which are being rebuilt, to the Elevador da Gloria, which takes us up to the Bairro Alto. This section of the city occupies its hill as if it were a world of its own. The quarter is a focal point in many ways. It derives its character from a mixture of everyday living, night life and business, the latter encompassing everything from begging to stylish designer boutiques. On weekends and in the high season there

is much pushing and shoving, since the most popular of the numerous fado clubs in Lisbon have also established themselves between the restaurants and trendy bars here. The rumour that this unique music is offered in a particularly authentic way, here of all places, holds persistently true.
Otherwise, for this part of Lisbon the following rule applies: follow the topography, since it reliably shows you the rewarding streets, the edges of which continue to be punctuated with surprises. In the Rua São Pedro de Alcantara, where we got out of the elevator, the small park of the miradouro of the same name, or the magnificent Port Wine Institute directly opposite, invite us to take a break, because a little further on to the west are the sumptuous green parks of the Praça do Principe Real. The Rua da Escola Politecnica leads on past the Academy Museum and the Botanical Garden into the lively business quarter, Rato. Despite the heavy traffic, with its pervasive roar and accompanying fumes, the largo still boasts tranquil residential side streets, where the hectic pace seems to disappear.
We will spurn the capricious shopping centre of Amoreiras and instead turn towards the western part of the city and the Estrela church. Directly in front is the park of the same name, the most lively of all Lisbon's green spaces. The Basilica da Estrela, built between 1776 and 1789 in commemoration of Maria I bearing a male successor to the throne, is the most important late Baroque church in the city. Its broad façade flanked by two towers is impressive, but even more so the high dome, accessible as a vantage point and also contributing to the clear structure of the single-aisled, bright interior of the church.
We now turn downhill again and go in an easterly direction. This is where the splendid electric tram line 28 begins, roaring down by the Palácio de São Bento, the seat of the Portuguese parliament, through the Calcada da Combro, before climbing steeply uphill once more. We are in the Bairro Alto again, but this time in its more elegant section. Several side streets, such as the Rua do Seculo, have quite an aristocratic character. Government offices, the school of music and the constitutional court all reside here, which is naturally reflected in the prices of the restaurants in the area. A stone's

Amoreiras-Shopping-Center

Amoreiras Shopping Center
below:
Basilica da Estrela
left:
View of the church from the Jardim da Estrela

throw away to the south lies the sunny Miradouro de Santa Catarina with a view of the docks of Santos and Alcantara. Just two streets further on we come to the tracks of another sloping lift, the yellow cabins of which spend an entire lifetime faithfully running up and down the steep incline. The Elevador da Bica is a vital line of communication that gives the street of the same name and its adjoining alleyways the status of an independent quarter. It even has a proper station house on the lower end of the Rua de São Paulo.

On the beautiful Praça Luis de Camoes our tour of the Chiado comes to an end. Close to here on 25 April 1974 thousands of Lisboans gathered in front of the police headquarters, singing, clapping and placing carnations, the symbol of their revolution, into the police rifles to celebrate the end of the dictatorship of Salazar, which had lasted over 40 years.

We now turn right into the Rua do Alecrim and reach the junction at Cais do Sodré. The station for trains to Estoril and Cascias is located here and behind it the landing-piers for the car ferries to Cacilhas on the opposite bank of the Tagus as well as Lisbon's largest market hall, the Ribeira Nova.

above and right page:
Transverse streets in
Bairro Alto
below:
Rua de São Paolo

In spite of the seasonal streams of tourists Lisbon still belongs to its inhabitants
right page: View from the Praça Luis de Camoes towards the Tagus

P
CONSULADO

above:
Palácio da Assembleia Nacional (São Bento)
below:
Aqueduct close to Serafina and streets
in Bairro Alto

left page:
Rua and Igreja de São Paolo

Chilean

Market scenes in the Ribeira Nova

Monument to the
Marques de Pombal

Nocturnal magic of the city

Elevadores and Electric Trams

Lisbon's public transportation system, in contrast to those of most other large cities, gives hardly any cause for anger or critique. True, the underground system with its one and a half lines is not particularly efficient – although it is to be upgraded for EXPO '98 – and the buses hold their own hardly better than anywhere else. But trams and cable cars provide local transportation of high quality, and also in the truest literal sense of the word.

Raoul Mesnier de Ponsard, the creator of the Elevador de Santa Justa, is also responsible for the construction of the Elevador da Bica that was put into operation in 1892, ten years before the photogenic luxury elevator in the city center. The other cable cars are even older. The Elevador da Gloria has been running since 1885 and the Elevador de Lavra, which is north of Rossio and hidden in the cliff, for even one year longer. This impeccable means of transportation is absolutely predestined for the trip to a secluded rendezvous in the Jardim de Torel!

Whereas water once provided the energy for the cable car, the predecessors of the tram were drawn by horses. Until the end of the last century, passengers were carried by partially track-guided wagons. In 1901 a hard-working fleet of electric trams was put into service and is still in use today.

Take a ride on tram line 28 and you will understand why. The wood paneling shines in the comfortable interior of this old electric tram and the chrome fittings glisten in the driver's cabin. The regular passengers greet one another and enjoy the short spurts of acceleration from one stop to the next by the open window. But it can also come to pass that the quick trip is suddenly interrupted by an unscheduled stop. Short-term parking on the tram tracks, Lisbon's number one peccadillo, often causes traffic jams which are likely to be solved in a sporty way. It only takes six, eight or ten hands to carry away a small car...

left page:
Elevador da Gloria
below:
A tram "doing its thing"

Lisbon's elevadores and electric trams may run a little sporadically at times, but they seem to enjoy an endlessly good reputation. It is hard to imagine more loyal allies than their clientele, the pedestrians. Just ask the little kids who like to ride along on the running-boards; they could tell you a thing or two.

The Miradouros

Lisbon is full of unexpected rewards. Even more characteristic than the elevadores and the trams are the city's miradouros, sights that are truly worthy of being seen. These small parks are always simply, but effectively designed in the best hilly locations that really do have the golden view that the name promises. And then there is the indisputable fact that here, you are above the small problems of life. Lingering in a miradouro helps you clear your mind and all the fresh air spurs on your well-being.
An especially picturesque example is the miradouro Santa Luzia, halfway up the mountain and offering an unforgettable panorama of the hills of the Alfama and, from time to time, the shimmering yellow "Sea of Straw" of the Tagus. But what should you admire more? This fantastic view? The captivating grounds of the miradouro with its walls, niches and balustrades decorated with tiles and entwined with plants? Or the composure of the old Lisboans, who regard the parade of tourists without batting an eye or better yet don't even look up from their round of dominos when a new busload of miradouro novices enter the scene? In the same way, these veterans are unwilling to let their game be interrupted in the winter, when this or the other rain shower comes. As experienced actors they are all, without exception, armed with immaculate umbrellas.
It almost looks as if Lisbon's miradouros were competing with each other for the most points, in terms of exposed location, worthwhile view, tiled explanatory signs, seating and ambience. The miradouros of Graça and Nossa Senhora do Monte, which due to their isolated locations are not as well-visited as the one of Santa Luzia, enjoy their quiet cult status nevertheless. Busier on the other hand, but also much larger, is the Miradouro São Pedro da Alcantara on the other side of the valley, which also had the honour of being the oldest of its species. Located on the south side of the Bairro

Favorite meeting place: the Miradouro Santa Luzia

Alto is the Miradouro de Santa Catarina, one of Lisbon's loveliest sun terraces. In addition, the small square is guarded by an impressive sculpture that shows the Adamastor, an allegorical figure from "The Lusiads", the Portuguese national poem by Luis de Camoes (c. 1524-1580).
There are certainly several more points in Lisbon that could make a claim to the title of miradouro due to their lay-out or view, for example the terraced square on the east end of the castle or the beautiful area below the aforementioned Jardim de Torel, where the evening view over the rooftops dives into the gilded heart of the city centre: the ideal spot to make wishes or to foster their fulfillment.

left page:
Adamastor near the
Miradouro de Santa Catarina
below:
Azulejo on the grounds of the
Miradouro Santa Luzia

Pavements, azulejos and big art

Is there need of any more proof that in this city the eye is flattered wherever you look? Usually of course, it is glued to the ground, since one is constantly faced with a steep upward or downward slope.

For this reason it seems logical that all of Lisbon's streets have handsome street pavements. Sometimes the decorative patterns are lovely enough to make you break into dance. The ornaments on the dead-straight avenida may be especially flowing, but in front of the entrances of offices they often become functional and even display names. Has the VW emblem ever looked better than in the pavement in front of the authorised dealership located in the Rato quarter?

Even more popular in Lisbon are the ubiquitous wall tiles, a fact which is proved by the immediate competitor of the "Auto Palace" near the Largo da Rato. Whoever studies the impressive glass and iron façade will also discover in it colourful tiles and indeed absolute jewels of art nouveau. From small treasures to atrocities, Lisbon is full of azulejos. The ceramic mosaics decorate interior as well as exterior walls and their motifs derive from traditional folk art and sometimes from contemporary design.

The tradition of tile painting is of Moorish and therefore Islamic origin, but in Portugal it did not remain limited to mere ornamentation for long. The name azulejo has, incidentally, nothing to do with the prominence of blue tones, but is based on the Arabic word for "small polished stone". The techniques of Moorish, Italian and Flemish masters were combined into a specifically Portuguese style starting in the mid-sixteenth century. From this time on the designs came to be characterised by an opulent colourfulness and a high-spirited tendency towards monumentality. Azulejos were incorporated more and more into the programmes of public buildings, motifs were derived from the history of the city, and tiles were even designed as

left page:
Cloister in the Igreja de São Vicente
below: Craft work for a profane cause

Alfama
AOS PÉS DE SANTA LUZIA ANINHA-SE A ALFAMA -
-COM OS TELHADOS EM PERGULA CONTÍNUA : AQUI UM
FRAGMENTO DE ÁGUA-FORTE, ALÉM UM PEDAÇO DE ÁGUA-
RELA. DESTE CENÁRIO ALFAMISTA, CINZENTO, SALPICADO
DE ROSA E VERDE-ERVILHA, ASCENDE A FRONTARIA BRANCA
DE SANTO ESTEVÃO, COMO QUE A ABENÇOAR AQUELA ME-
DIANIA URBANISTA, DELIRANTE DE LABIRINTOS.
NORBERTO DE ARAUJO « LEGENDAS DE LISBOA
Duas sugestões
para visita
CML

information plaques with overviews and explanatory keys.

The most famous tiles are kept in the National Tile Museum in the convent of Madre de Deus, which contains the world's largest collection. The most important piece is a 40 metre-long wall frieze that shows Lisbon before the devastating earthquake of 1755.

Of the many museums, each of which is exhaustively and devotedly committed to its special field, the Fundação Gulbenkian plays a very special role. The bequest of Caslouste Sarkis Gulbenkian (1869-1955), an oil magnate of Armenian descent who in 1942 emigrated from Great Britain to the capital of neutral Portugal, has long since become the decisive cultural factor in Lisbon. Its not unproblematic position of monopoly can hardly be challenged by newer institutions such as the Centro Cultural located in Belém.

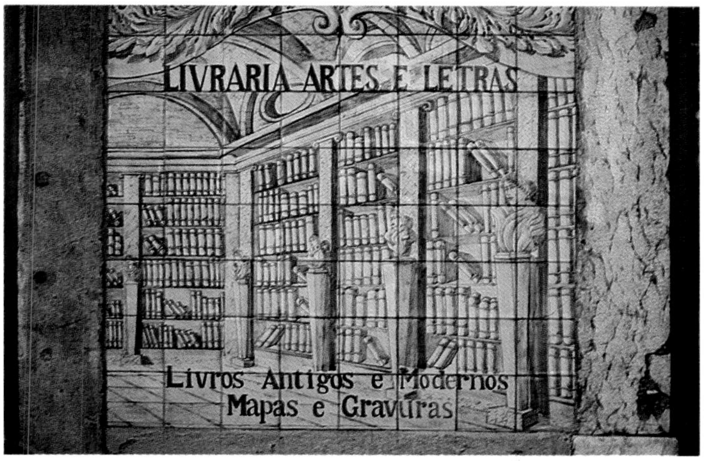

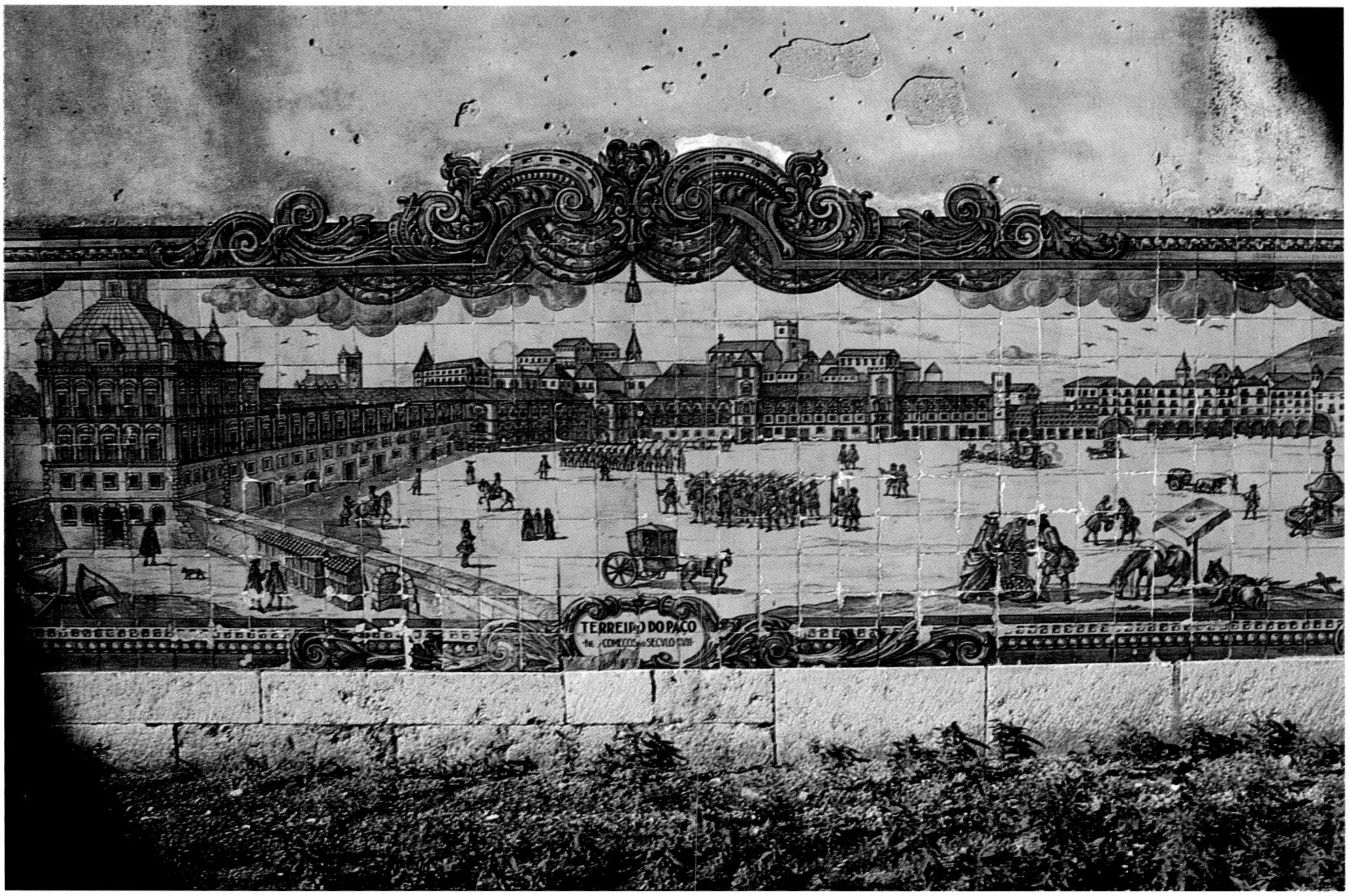

Examples of azulejo decoration on the walls and pavements of Lisbon

The grounds not only accommodate the Gulbenkian Museum and the Centre of Modern Art with their important collections, but also a garden with a sculpture park and an amphitheatre.
In addition the Gulbenkian Foundation has supported its own symphony orchestra with a choir and ballet since the sixties. Because this cultural field appeared to be the least suspect, Portugal's musical life was able to flourish decisively during the Salazar era. The Gulbenkian Library also sent out important impulses, so that meanwhile a network of more than a total of 200 branches in the whole country exists.

Amphitheatre in the museum park of the Gulbenkian Foundation

BIBLIOTECA JARDIM
CULTURA

Green Squares, Parks and Gardens

Its little walls and steps make Lisbon often appear like a stone garden. A multitude of shady squares in the middle of the maze of houses and in front of the numerous churches invites you to pause. Yet the city also contains many green oases, most of which are absolutely worthy of a separate trip. The botanical garden, which can be reached from the east by the Rua da Alegria or, coming from Rato, by the Rua da Escola Politecnica, is regarded as one of the most beautiful ones in Europe. In a relatively small space on a lushly wooded slope, it surprises with many rare plants from all over the world. In the upper area an impressive dragon tree from the islands of Cape Verde especially draws attention to itself and questions the right of all the other palm trees to the beauty prize.
Museum-like in comparison, but no less fascinating is the Estufa Fria, the "cold greenhouse", on the northwesterly end of the monumental Parque Eduardo VII above the rotunda. This garden complex was laid out in 1929 for local and tropical plants and has a rather temple-like character. And under the transparent wooden roof a steady temperature and guaranteed tropical conditions are maintained all year round, a climate nevertheless quite mild for its clientele.
Of the small parks the Principe Real on the square of the same name is especially worth mentioning, even if only for its Lusitanian cypress which has a

Impressions from the Estufa Fria and the Jardim da Estrela

crown measuring an impressive 2.5 metres. The Jardim da Estrela, considered the most beautiful of the larger parks, is where the inhabitants of the western part of the city get their fill of chlorophyll and oxygen. This green plateau is a favourite site for relaxing by all the rules of the game, from a refreshing, quick rest in-between appointments to a leisurely lounge of a few hours in agreeable half-shadow.

Those staying for longer in Lisbon should take the time to visit the park of the Palácio de São Bento or the botanical garden in Belém with the lovely name Jardim do Ultramar. The so-called Parque Florestal de Monsanto was originally conceived as a "green lung" for the city, but today this wooded area is spoiled and hardly worth the trip. On the other hand, the lovely Jardim de Torel already mentioned is to be recommended, even on a short visit to Lisbon. That way you will not be forced to settle for the parks along the Avenida da Liberdade, which are nevertheless fitted out with little squares and street cafés.

left page:
The founder of the Botanical Garden watches over his grounds
below left:
Street café on the Avenida da Liberdade

below right:
Idleness in the Jardim da Estrela
Following double-page:
In the Estufa Fria

PAIO

Pastelarias: Heaven on Earth

Even as a pedestrian your pace is often too quick to catch the surprising vistas along the narrow streets, boldly decorated portals, mysterious shops and shadowy patios. But a plate filled with fresh, colourful pastries that were just placed in the window of a pastelaria can cause you to slam on the brakes.

The fact that the colourful goings-on in these establishments are taken for granted makes them appear all the more enticing to foreigners. A pastelaria serves dozens of everyday functions for all types of people. At the counter, passers-by take their bica, a Portuguese espresso. Groups of school children tend to leave the floor looking like a battlefield strewn with sweet wrappers. A woman engrossed in a novel sweetens her reading with a few pasteis at a little table. A street worker propped on his shovel

left page above:
Padaria in the Rua Dom Pedro V
left page below:
Typical pub in the Baixa
below:
Street café on the Campo Cebolas

in the doorway downs a glass of port. Also a waitress from the neighbouring pension, who has just finished cranking out continental breakfast, finds refuge, along with a desperately needed, proper coffee and a chat with her workmates.

Everybody here, from the regulars to the one-time visitors, is served according to their individual needs and habits. It is difficult to think of a more appropriate place than a nice pastelaria to study the theory and practice of physical and mental well-being.

But the culinary offering is usually not limited to those things you would expect in a good café. In addition to the famous pastry which Portuguese cuisine has developed into an extravagant diversity of tastes, at least a tasty soup of the day is also to be had in just about any pastelaria. And at midday, especially in the inner city, bars have several dishes on offer that are meals in themselves. These are served according to the individual schedules of the customers. In addition, Lisbon has hundreds of restaurants, and especially in Alfama the density cannot be bettered. Most of them specialise in fish and even in the simplest restaurants you can make culinary discoveries.

The Old Gate to the New World

Belém

After our walks around the inner city, it is time for a trip to the suburb of Belém which is located five kilometres away. Given the distance we have already walked and the amount this former fishing village has to offer, you should allow at least half a day for this excursion and take the tram. This follows a varied route at a more leisurely pace than the coastal express train, and gives at least a few of the many surprises along the way the chance to make a fleeting impression, like the tram depot in the shadow of an enormous pilaster of the Ponte 25 Abril just before Santo Amaro.

Even before we reach Belém the scenery changes completely: small-town buildings assert themselves bravely next to imposing palaces that are allowed to take up immense areas here. The Palácio de Belém, formerly a royal country estate, is today the official seat of the state president. The former riding school bustles daily with the busloads of tourists who come to visit the Coach Museum. Standing on the symmetrical Praça do Imperio with the Fonte Luminoso in its middle, we are now exactly on the spot where Portugal's fame as a seafaring nation began. In 1415 young Prince Henry embarked from here with 240 ships to conquer the coast of North Africa. Hundreds of journeys were to follow: the crusades, expeditions of discovery, colonisation and trade, all of which were to increase Portugal's riches.

Standing majestically on the long side of the spacious square, the Mosteiro dos Jerónimos surpasses even the highest expectations that you might have had just from the photographs. This overwhelming effect is certainly what the builders of the Manueline architecture intended when they enriched late Gothic elements with wild naturalism. The fine details are reminiscent of silver jewellery, held under control with a sovereign sense for the effect of the whole. King Manuel I ordered the monastery to be built in 1502, during Portugal's golden age as a naval power, in honour of Vasco

left page:
Praça do Imperio with the Mosteiro dos Jerónimos
below:
Manueline details

left page:
Igreja Santa Maria, the richly decorated south portal
above left:
Main choir from the Renaissance
below left:
Gothic net-vaulting
below right:
Octagonal cupola tower
following double-page:
Cloister

In the cloister

da Gama, who had successfully returned from India. Even today the Mosteiro dos Jerónimos is architecturally and historically one of the most important buildings in the country. The monastery cloister, a product of Manueline architecture in its purest form, and the interior of the three-aisled church of Santa Maria, are unforgetably beautiful and impress every time anew.

Emerging from the solemn coolness and the almost cave-like darkness into the square again, the contrast could hardly be more abrupt. On the west side of the park complex, exposed to the intense light without protection, stands the newly built Centro Cultural de Belém, an unapproachable, modernist fortress. Yet what could be a more effective counterbalance to the 300 metre long Jerónimo monastery and a credible connection to the discoverer monument on the Tagus promenade than this awe-inspiring block of red limestone? Although this exhibition and concert centre is devoted to the fine arts on an international level today, its original purpose and its source of financing is obvious. After completion in 1992 it housed the rotating EC chairmanship for half a year.

On the Padrão dos Descobrimentos, a fairly plain lump of concrete more than fifty metres high, Portugal's explorer-heroes are immortalised. First and foremost is Henry the Seafarer, whose monument was dedicated in 1960 by Salazar himself, marking the occasion of the explorer's death 500 years earlier. A lift on the inside of the stylised ship's bow leads to the observation platform, where, in the form of a mosaic on the square below, the whole world literally lays at your feet.

Centro Cultural de Belém

To complete the mandatory program we lack only one of the most prominent symbols of Lisbon, indeed the city's most familiar touristic advertising image. The Torre de Belém, built at the same time as the Mosteiro dos Jerónimos, is actually of surprisingly modest dimensions. In order that the block-like, yet richly and almost playfully decorated fortress tower might continue to stand in water as it always had, it was necessary to widen the Tagus artificially at this point. The five stories of the tower are well-preserved and their original functions can easily be guessed: dungeon, armoury, kitchen and dining room, one floor for the king and another

Padrão dos Descobrimentos and yacht harbour

LARA
CAPTAIN E

previous double-page:
Torre de Belém, general view
right, below and right page:
Details

for his court. A walk around the exterior is like taking a stroll with the royal entourage: minaret-like domes decorate the crown of the tower and all of the corners and the wall consoles are decorated with Manueline ornaments and artfully reproduced animal heads. Until the earthquake of 1755 the Torre de Belém had a twin on the opposite side of the Tagus river. Clearly the Portuguese Empire was quite concerned with receiving and bidding farewell to their allies and enemies alike, as befitted their social standing.

By now it is high time for coffee and cake! On good days hundreds of tourists and locals pay a visit to the traditional Pasteis de Belém on the main street leading to the Praça Afonso de Albuquerque, and with good cause. Afterwards, for a digestive walk, you can stroll past the tropical garden and the beautifully proportioned Igreja de São José da Memoria towards the hill of Restelo. The urbanisation of this area between Tagus and the woods of Monsanto was begun in 1940 as part of Salazar's fascist estado novo. Since the seventies this quarter has combined its privileged

location with well-ordered prosperity and today enjoys, even on the side away from the river, its status as a showpiece of city planning.
Running between the Restelo stadium and the Museum of Overseas Ethnology is the road to the Ermida Manuelina de São Jerónimo. Unfortunately the small chapel decorated with shells is usually closed, but from here is a fantastic view of Belém and the Torre. Behind it the shimmering Tagus dissolves almost furtively and without drama into the sea. To the right your gaze can wander unimpeded in the direction of the fashionable seaside towns of Estoril and Cascais and onward to the western end of Europe, a strangely sad piece of land before the immeasurable Atlantic.

Igreja de São José da Memoria

Lisbon has taught us that optimism settles further up the river, behind the safe harbour, and on the seven hills of the city – and recently once again on the banks of the Tagus, especially the former military and industrial zone on the Cabo Ruivo. This enormous area was practically predestined to be the location of EXPO '98 and is presently undergoing an enormous metamorphosis. Projects are now being completed around Europe's largest construction site – the title which is often incorrectly given to Potsdamer Platz in Berlin. These projects include the new bridge across the Tagus named after Vasco da Gama, additional underground stations, the new Train Station East and of course the pavilions of the 128 participating countries. These structures and other projects such as the long-planned train line for the Bridge of the 25th of April will be built largely by African immigrants from Portugal's former colonies. Jobs that are badly paid and often very dangerous are presently available here in some abundance.

At least Lisbon's economically inspired building projects are designed to be visually distinctive. But the globalisation, and the strict egalitarianism that comes with it, persistently ignore the social problems, only serving to make the situation worse.

Perhaps the most pressing question in the future will be to ask which forces Lisbon intends to mobilise after the world exhibition to assure its continued well-being!

Historical details

Pre-history Over one hundred stone age archeological sites prove that there is a densely populated settlement in the Lisbon area.

1100 BC The Phoenicians recognize the suitability of the Tagus as a natural harbour and make Lisbon a port of call on their trade routes with North Africa and Northern Europe, naming the city "alis-ubbo". They are succeeded by the Carthaginians and later by the Greeks.

218 BC The Romans begin to conquer Iberia. Thirteen years later they also occupy Lisbon, then known as "Olisipo", which becomes the capital of the newly formed province of Lusitania under Emperor Augustus.

From 400 AD Retreat of the Romans. Lisbon becomes part of the empire of the Visigoths, with the capital at Toledo.

587 The Visigoths under King Rekkared I convert to Christianity.

711 The North African army commander Tarik lands in Gibraltar. After three years Lisbon also becomes Arabic and now belongs to the Emirate of Cordoba.

From 750 The Christian reconquest of the Iberian peninsula, the so-called reconquista, starts from Galicia, the later kingdom of Léon.

868 Portucale, the area around Porto in the north of the country, falls to Léon.

1095 Henrique, count of Burgundy, receives Portucale as fief.

1128 His son Afonso I declares his independence from Léon and continues the reconquista.

1139 Afonso I declares himself king.

1147 Afonso conquers Lisbon in the course of the otherwise disastrous second crusade and in the same year lays the foundation-stone of Sé Patriarcal.

1179 His kingdom is recognized by the pope.

1250 With the conquest of Algarve the reconquista of Portugal is complete. Since then the country has existed in its present boundaries.

1256 The royal residence is moved from Coimbra to Lisbon.

1290 The university is founded in Lisbon, but is moved to Coimbra in 1307-08.

From 1300 Lisbon's importance grows as a trading port between the Mediterranean and Northern Europe and as an export harbour for fish, wood and salt. The reclamation of land begins on the Tagus. The city centre shifts from the hill of the fortress to the river bank.

1337 - 1347 Three serious earthquakes shake the city.

1348 As a result of the first plague epidemic many people flee from the countryside to Lisbon.

1383 King Fernão dies. His Spanish wife takes power and instigates a connection to Spain with the help of sections of the Portuguese nobility who see their role threatened by the growing power of the merchant class. But the Lisboans make João I their king.

1385 The Portuguese, supported by English troops, defeat the Castilians near Aljubarrota. Commanding with João is Nuno Alvares, who then founds the Convento do Carmo.

1415 Prince Henry the Seafarer takes part in the conquest of the North African seaport Ceuta. Thereafter he plans and organizes the search for the sea route that was believed to lead around the supposed southern tip of Africa to India. In this endeavor he uses all of the technical, scientific and financial means that he has access to, in order to assure the success of this naval expedition along the African coast.

1444 The first African slaves are sold in Lagos and Algarve.

1494 In the Treaty of Tordesillas Spain and Portugal agree to demarcate the border of their interests in the western hemisphere at 46 degrees longitude.

1498 Vasco da Gama finally lands in India, thirty-eight years after Prince Henry's death.

1500 Pedro Alvares Cabral makes it to Brazil. Along the newly discovered coast settlements are founded as trading bases, especially for the spice trade. Lisbon surpasses Venice and becomes the largest harbour in the world.

From 1502 Manuel I builds the Jerónimo Monastery in Belém with the huge profits from the spice trade.

1511 The residence is moved from the castle of São Jorge to a new palace on the present Praça do Comércio.

From 1513 The Bairro Alto is systematically urbanised.

1531 Earthquake.

1536 The Inquisition, the introduction of which Manuel I had bound himself to in a marriage contract, begins. The Jesuits are responsible for its implementation.

1540	The first execution takes place on the Rossio.
1547	The censors publish a list of forbidden books.
1569	The plague causes approximately 60,000 deaths.
1578	King Sebastião tries to conquer Morocco and perishes along with a large part of his army. In the same year the plague breaks out again for the last time.
1580	With the death of Henrique II the Avis dynasty dies out. The Spaniards occupy Portugal.
1588	The annihilation of the Spanish Armada by the English leads to the loss of many of Portugal's settlements overseas.
1640	A national uprising brings the duke of Bragança to the throne as João IV. He gains the support of England.
1688	Spain recognizes Portugal's borders.
1693	Discovery of large gold deposits in Brazil.
From 1706	King João V spends most of the new wealth on churches and palaces.
1748	The Alcantara aqueduct is dedicated.
From. 1750	The Marques de Pombal, as prime minister of José I, introduces sweeping reforms in the spirit of the Enlightenment and mercantilism.
1755	The great earthquake destroys large parts of the city.
1758	Pombal uses the assassination attempt on José I as an opportunity to expel the Jesuits.
1761	Slave trade is abolished.
1777	Maria I deprives Pombal of his power and annuls his reforms. She brings back the Jesuits. The revival of the inquisition breaks every resistance against the clerical reaction.
1794	The last sentence of the inquisition is carried out.
1807	With the help of the English Lisbon successfully defends itself against the French siege. The court flees to Brazil, which is released from the colonial relationship.
1820	The English military administration ends when the king returns. In Porto and Lisbon a liberal revolution breaks out.
1821	Portugal receives its first constitution.

1822	Brazil declares its independence. The resulting absence of gold deliveries causes Portugal to experience an economic crisis.
1828	King Miguel I annuls the constitution.
1832 - 34	The liberals gain acceptance in the civil war and send Miguel into exile. Monasteries and religious orders are disbanded.
1838	The first industrial exhibition takes place in Lisbon, the first worker's assembly is formed.
1856	The railway reaches Lisbon.
1869	Slavery is abolished.
1879	Construction of the Avenida da Liberdade is begun to expand the city to the north.
1884	The first cable car, the Elevador da Lavra is opened, and one year later the Elevador da Gloria.
1890	The first train arrives at Rossio Station.
1901	The first electric tram goes into operation.
1908	Carlos I, who had attempted to reign as a dictator, is murdered on the Praça do Comércio .
1910	The monarchy comes to an end and a republic is declared.
1911	The republican constitution comes into force.
1916 - 18	Portugal participates in World War I.
1919 - 20	The world economic crisis leads to unrest and strikes.
1926	Military coup overthrows the forty-fifth republican government in sixteen years. The parliament is dissolved and the constitution is annulled.
1928	António de Oliveira Salazar becomes minister of finance under President General Carmona. He restores the national finances by drastic budget cuts. Opposition is brutally suppressed.
1933	Salazar lets his plan of a fascist Estado Novo based on Italian and German models be confirmed by a plebiscite. Inner repression and outer isolation become the dominant elements of Portuguese politics.
1936 - 45	Portugal remains neutral in the Spanish Civil War and in World War II.
1940	The dictatorship celebrates itself in an "Exhibition of the Portuguese World" in Belém to establish links with its glorious past.
1949	Portugal is a charter member of NATO.
1959	The grand opening of the first section of the underground.
1960	The Discoveries Monument in Belém is dedicated.
1961	War begins against the liberation movements in Angola and Mozambique.
1966	The bridge over the Tagus is completed.
1970	Salazar dies. His successor is Marcelo Caetano.
1974	The attempt by the military to take over power provokes the Revolution of the Carnations.
1975	The colonies are allowed to become independent. Hundreds of thousands return to Portugal.
1976	The socialist constitution is retired.
1986	Portugal, along with Spain, becomes a member of the EC.
1994	Lisbon is cultural capital of Europe.
1998	Lisbon is host to the world exhibition EXPO.

Text
Andreas Schäfler

Editorial & Historical Details
Gabriela Wachter

Translation
Tas Skorupa

Layout & Typesetting
Gabriela Wachter

Special thanks to Bernhard Meyer, Rosa Schädler and Christoph Weber

Photo sources

Archiv für Kunst und Geschichte, Berlin:
page 17 (lower), page 22
Andreas Schäfler:
Page 30, page 63 (both), page 68 (lower), page 76, backcover
Gabriela Wachter:
Page 7 (all), page 11, page 18 (below), page 19 (below), page 24, page 26, page 29 (lower), page 36 (lower), page 37 (both), page 46 (lower), page 49, page 51 (lower middle left), page 53 (both above and middle, left and lower), page 58 (lower right), page 62, page 64 (lower), page 66 (above left), page 67, page 68 (above left), page 70, page 72, page 74 (both), page 75, page 77 (both), page 78 (lower), page 81 (lower right), page 82, page 84 (both)
Klaus Carl:
Front jacket, page 1, page 8, page 9, page 12, page 13, page 17 (above), page 18 (above), page 27 (both), page 28, page 29 (both above), page 31 (both), page 33 (below), page 34 (above, middle left and below, both), page 36 (above), page 45 (above), page 48 (both above, middle left and lower right), page 52, page 53 (middle left), page 58 (above, middle and lower left), page 59 (below), page 60 (above), page 64 (above), page 65 (all), page 66 (below), page 71 (left), page 78 (above), page 79, page 80(both), page 81 (left, both), page 85, page 88, page 90 (all), page 91
Ulli Schmidt:
Pages 2, 4, 5, 6 (both), page 10, page 14, page 15 (all), page 16 (both), page 19 (above), page 20 (both), page 21, page 29 (middle), page 32 (both), page 33 (above), page 34 (middle right), page 35 (both), page 38 (both), page 39 (both), page 40, page 42 (all), page 43 (both), page 44, page 45 (below), page 46 (above), page 47, page 48 (middle and lower left), page 50, page 51 (above), (lower left and lower middle left, and lower right), page 54 (both), page 55 (all), page 56, page 57, page 59 (above), page 60 (middle and lower), page 61, page 66 (above right), page 68 (above middle, both; and above right), page 71 (right), page 86 (both), page 87 (all), page 92

4-12 Old Christchurch Road
Bournemouth BH1 1LG, England

ISBN 1 85995 370 0